Not Much to Say Really

Kelvin Corcoran
& Emma Collins

Not Much to Say Really

*4 Solo Voices
and a chorus*

Shearsman Books

First published in the United Kingdom in 2017 by
Shearsman Books
50 Westons Hill Drive
Emersons Green
BRISTOL
BS16 7DF

Shearsman Books Ltd Registered Office
30–31 St. James Place, Mangotsfield, Bristol BS16 9JB
(this address not for correspondence)

www.shearsman.com

ISBN 978-1-84861-559-5

Contents

Foreword

Junior doctors still wore white coats back then, pockets filling with books and stethoscopes and lists so that the cloth pulled at our shoulders. Despite this weight, the coats lifted like capes as we rounded corners or strode hurriedly through corridors. Buoyed perhaps, at least in our minds' eye, by some belief in medicine's heroism, how we all held such sway over life and death. That afternoon I was stood with my consultant in his office discussing career plans. I'm thinking about about elderly care, I said, or maybe oncology. He peered over his glasses and told me to set my sights on oncology. Choose a specialty, he said, where there's proper science, one where you can make an actual difference to patients' lives.

Of course science informs medicine, and armed with it doctors of all disciplines make a real difference to patients' lives. But the science isn't enough. And our emphasis on it leaves us with a limited and limiting conception of medicine. One inflated by hubris and in such denial of human mortality, one impoverished so often of moral judgment, and one that sidesteps the human encounter at the heart of all medicine. Human encounter that's loaded at its best with empathy, that renders others' suffering as palpable and that compels us to act well.

Medicine that dwells almost monochromatically on the technically possible will too quickly disregard the needs of the elderly. It objectifies them to a nuisance of discharge or placement. Or it reductively medicalises the final years of life without attention to quality or the wider aspects of patient care. How is this still possible in the twenty-first century? What does it say about a society's values?

Medicine Unboxed is a project that asks just these questions of society and healthcare. Medicine is practiced and received now in the context of extraordinary scientific knowledge and therapeutic prowess, but it faces increasing moral, political and social challenges. We believe the arts and humanities can illuminate these challenges, drawing us into conversation, fostering awe, wonder, and perhaps even humility.

We asked the poet, Kelvin Corcoran and the doctor and artist, Emma Collins to meet and speak with elderly patients in Cheltenham General Hospital, then to translate these conversations into creative works. The poems and artworks in this book offer us a glimpse of other human lives; of persons who have experienced our very own desires, fears and hopes; of human beings who are now briefly patients. Patients who we owe a duty beyond the delivery of just blood tests or drugs or suitable placement. Patients and persons who, one day soon, we ourselves will be.

Dr Sam Guglani
Consultant Oncologist
Director, Medicine Unboxed
Cheltenham
9 April 2017

Introduction

Kelvin Corcoran

'nothing matters but the quality
of the affection—
in the end—that has carved the trace in the mind
dove sta memoria'
(Ezra Pound, Canto LXXVI)

For a number of months in 2014 and 2015 I spent time talking and listening to elderly patients in Cheltenham General Hospital. I was invited to do this as part of a Medicine Unboxed project called 'Showing Your Age' curated by Dr. Sam Guglani. The patients' first reaction was pretty much always the same—*Well, there's not much to say really.* Then the talk would come pouring out. I listened to more people than are included here. Some did not want to be recorded, some moved on from the hospital and others died. I met and talked to Joan, Doris, John and Elizabeth several times before finally recording any of our conversations. Mostly I listened, went home and thought about what I'd heard.

What is written here is not simple transcription, though these are the words of the four speakers. I've edited and joined together different moments of conversations with the same speaker. I've also shaped the writing to the individual voices in several ways. This is not just a matter of idiolect but also how the typical rhythm of an individual's speech carries thought, feeling and characteristic wit. For instance, Joan spoke in rounded almost epigrammatic phrases but in short bursts. Her medical condition meant she was short of breath but also she was thinking deeply about what she said. She was summing up her life, as were the other three speakers.

There is another principle shaping the written accounts here, one discovered as I went along. There is of course an awareness on the part of each speaker of looking back and weighing up the life lived. However, in the heart of this process, it became apparent that much of the conversation for each speaker swung around a few cardinal, unavoidable experiences. They were the experiences which drew thought like the pull of gravity, the points to which thinking and unfinished feeling returned. These moments of vulnerability and realisation are perfectly reflected in Emma Collins' illustrations. Sometimes, at first, these moments were only partly acknowledged but at other times they were seen plainly and spoken about directly. They were the things never for-gotten and still to be considered because they were always there. The importance of such feeling 'carved in the trace of the mind' explains why the text is arranged as four solo voices followed by a chorus. As deeply personal and intimate as these central experiences were for each speaker, they were also the experiences completely shared from one person to another, the points at which the deepest and most individual feelings are the common lot we live. This is why the solo voices come together as a choir in chorus.

I was able to hear these voices, and how much they had to say, because of the work and kindness of Dr. Helen Alexander and her colleagues. So *Not Much To Say Really* is for them and in appreciation of the life stories told by Joan, Doris, John and Elizabeth.

EMMA COLLINS

I was delighted to be asked to be part of this collaborative project, initiated by Care of the Elderly consultant at Cheltenham General Hospital, Dr. Helen Alexander, and Dr. Samir Guglani. The aim of the project was to give a voice to elderly patients in a hospital setting. During my time in hospital medicine, I unfortunately encountered many people who lost their identity as soon as they entered the hospital bed: their stories and personalities were masked by their disease, their test results, and the endless clinical tasks that are assigned to them. People can easily become defined by their disease, which can have a de-humanising effect. Some healthcare professionals may find this method of distancing themselves from the patient a way to stay focused, or a coping mechanism to protect themselves from the stresses and responsibilities of the job. But in order to deliver true holistic, patient-centred care, it is so important to acknowledge the patient as a person with a rich and complex history that we could learn a great deal from, if we spent the time to engage in their narratives. Anecdotally, it has been found that elderly patients who bring in pictures of themselves when they were younger to adorn their bedside are often treated differently by their care-givers, as it sparks off conversations that breaks down the boundaries established through the roles of patient and health care provider.

I used the written transcripts of the conversations between the patients and Kelvin as a starting point for my work. I was deeply moved reading them. Although I did not meet these people, I got a real sense of their personalities reading them. I was struck by how honest and open their accounts were. Some were melancholic; others were a true celebration of a life well spent. Some reflected on the process of aging that they were acutely experiencing, and the incomprehensible changes they had witnessed. Others concentrated on their past. They are four very different people, but what unifies them is the unsettling environment that they find themselves in. This unifying quality is represented in the work through the muted tones used, reflecting the uniformity of the ward itself.

The transcripts offered a small insight into personal memories, and I have illustrated these fragmented images to represent each individual. The narrative connotations of fabric and thread compliment the delicacy and vulnerability of the memories, mirrored by the layering and fraying of the textiles themselves. The physical presence of fabric has several intimate associations with people over the course of a lifetime: it being the first thing that wraps us up and protects us at birth, and the last thing to touch our skin before death. To emphasise this point, textiles, such as handkerchiefs, have been used to connect the memories with tangible, day-to-day objects.

The translucency of the fabrics used not only highlights the fragility of the patients and their memories, but also represents the lack of privacy experienced by the patients, despite the best intentions of staff. This was clear from reading the transcripts, where intimate thoughts, perhaps never before spoken out loud in one case, were abruptly interrupted by shouts from another patient in a neighbouring bed, or a nurse bustling in to take a set of observations.

The text used in the images are the exact words used by the patients themselves from the transcripts.

We had all the
wouldn't give in

Four Figures Sing for Life
from the White Sheets of Final Care

I was born in 1930 – I married when?
then the war, but the children never came,
my brother died when I was ten,
it regrets me still, that something unfinished.

I was their eldest daughter's mistake;
three sons I had and my husband died,
you had a handful people said – but no
I loved them and it was a pleasure.

Well that was me working on the farm,
me and my dad, up the hills, the best school;
though she left me, I love her even still
oh but my daughter's the pillar of my life.

The year? I don't remember. I'll ask Tony,
ah – no, I can't can I, he's gone now, hmm,
but we had fun, hungry most of the war,
the Mediterranean, salt water out of the taps.

Three women and a man sing for life
moment by moment from their beating hearts;
the miracle of ordinary events recalled
– oh but I miss him, all gone now I know.

everything's changed
the things people have now
we couldn't afford

272342

Four Solo Voices

Joan

Joan, you said a few minutes ago, there's not much to say really.

No, ha, well, ha, I was,
I was born January 16th 1930.
I was born at the Air Balloon,
do you know the Air Balloon?
– but not the pub.

My dad worked on an estate.

It was bad times then, you know.

He had Jim George Tony and then me.
but that wasn't the finish
after I was born there was Mari,
then there was John then there was little Alan
he died at 14 months – and then Ann, 8 of us.

What happened, she was expecting him in the war time
my mother was up at the window
doing the blackout and fell back, well anyway
he was born with a big dog's bone like, a hair lip
his nose went straight across there, no pallet.

He was in the children's hospital in London
for his operations, they used to go up by taxi, to see him.
Alan would have been … 74 now.
He was there all the time, the war was on,
before the NHS, dad was in a club.

In those days your mum nor your dad
never told you much, do you know what I mean?
Where you were born was just under a gooseberry bush.
Anyway he came, they brought him home,
he had just a little red line there, he had a new pallet, a new gum
a new nose, well, they done it all.

We said, oh don't let him go back, don't let him go back again,
they said he's got to go back, just for a fortnight.
He developed pneumonia and died.
What it was it was terrible, terrible.
Time doesn't… It doesn't no, no it never does.

I don't think they're ever, when I say gone,
we know they're gone, it's the same with mum and dad
I still talk to mum and dad, when I go down to the graves,
the stones like, I'm always talking to them.
The sting doesn't go away. No, no it doesn't.

*

I think, if I'd have been born later
I might have been able to get a little bit more in here
but I didn't and that was it. I was 14 when I left school
left on the Friday, work on the Monday.

I can remember not being able to learn properly
it was awful, I couldn't seem to take things in
and this is what, it regrets me now
I wish I could have took it all in.

Of course the war was on, so we didn't do much,
the children were from Birmingham, I think,
they came to our school and we all caught head lice
but anyway, mum soon got rid of it.

*

My husband? I met him when I was – 16, 17
A sweet young thing then? Yes. And he came from Yorkshire
to work on the farm and then he went back
but we wrote to each other and we got married.

We lived in a cottage on the manor estate
and Alan's boss's wife said Joan – would you like to help me?
I said yes and I was there 48 years and enjoyed it all,
of course they had their children and they still come to see me.

I saw them grow up. I enjoyed all that part.
My sister had Nigel and was expecting again
and she said I don't know how to tell Joan
because at that time we were trying for a child.

No no we never had children in the end,
I had these tests, it was looked into, there was no reason,
they gave me tablets but they didn't do any good,
I just didn't make the eggs and they didn't catch on.

So that was that but anyway I had … I enjoyed
my sister's, I loved her little one and took him everywhere
my other sister had two boys, and the children from the manor.

Time. They've gone now. There's only John, my younger sister
and me that's living now…
                                   Any hot drinks?
        No I don't think so love.

*

When you think back and see how things are now,
what strikes you as the big changes?

Everything's changed, everything's changed
the things people have now, we couldn't afford.
My dad always said to me, he used to call me, my wench –
my wench, he said, don't you get buying anything, he said,
unless you can afford it because it will get you into trouble.

We never had newspapers to read, it was just Dandies
and that wasn't very often, so of course you didn't hear a lot.
The world does bother me now, I think oh my golly,
our neighbour she's expecting a baby and I think
oh dear what's that little lad going to come into, you know.

It nearly breaks your heart, it really does, but then, there again,
I mean, she loves that little girl, I've never seen a mother like it.

Of course we never had the clothes you can have today,
you know I was 16 and I was still wearing my gabardine coat
that I wore at school, mum never ever turned down parcels,
there was, and I can remember, she had a lovely parcel come,
it was a beautiful coat and I had that for ages and absolutely loved it.

I was working but for very little money, oh dear, 1/6d an hour,
we never got in debt, when Alan first went on the farm,
he only got £5, you see £5 a week, which was nothing.
It's unbelievable now. It is, it is. A cup of coffee and a cake.
Oh true true. *And you were living on that.* Yes.

Hello, good afternoon, here we are.

Oh thank you very much.

Joan I'm going to let you eat your lunch in peace.

little Alan died at fourteen months

my brother
would have been
seventy jan...

he was born with a big pigeon bone
like a bird lip
his nose went straight across
no palate

He was in the children's hospital for his operations. they made ... and washing
we said don't let him go back again they said he's got to go back just for a fortnight
he developed pneumonia and died what it was it was terrible terrible
time doesn't — no it never does

it's like when I saw the doctor

last year, he said was an advert

he said

for other people

I accept my diagnosis?

I said keep smiling

keep working

and a bit of a wrinkle

wear

I think I won't do it now

Doris

I was born in 1922, 2.11.22. I went to an ordinary school. I'd passed the scholarship but I was brought up by my grandfather and he wouldn't let me go to the grammar school. He wouldn't let his own daughters go either, he didn't believe in it.

Because you were girls?

No he was a farmer and he thought it was a waste of time. He was a farmer in Lincolnshire. Do you know on Friday it's twenty years since my second husband died? I was so worried coming here in case I spoiled my boys' Christmas, if anything happened. They tell me not to worry. It's as if I knew. I did 23 Christmas cakes, I do them for the hospital in Cirencester, I've done them for ten years. I've done them for this hospital when I was in Cheltenham. And the doctors warned them and that and my son's got them all done, he's got to collect a couple now and the whole 23 has gone. And I look around here and I think this place is beautiful. Perhaps I helped a little bit. I like making people happy, it makes me happy and it makes them happy.

Yes. So I left at 14 and went to work, I worked in an arts and crafts shop. And then in 1942 I married my first husband. And then I travelled around a little, went to Felixstowe and got a job in a big store. And before that I was a nanny to some little children, I was 16.

I'm just taking these, is that ok Doris?

Oh yes, thank you lovey, I'd be grateful for that.

We were married in '42 and Phillip was born in '46. And then I had three in 7 years 2 months, three boys. People say, quite a handful but no. My biggest ambition was to have a child of my own – and I made them a pleasure. And we were short of money so I ran a guest house, so they didn't go short of anything. When they were off from school I was home and when they were poorly I was home. In them days there weren't nursery schools around. Of course when I was younger you never heard of anyone having a baby at 40 or anything like that.

Am I in the way?

No, no don't worry.

It's spotlessly clean and I love the white linen. I keep my sheets like that. My sons can't get over the kindness of the nurses in here.

*

You know my sister used to say, I'll take Phillip out. I'd say no, he's alright. She used to say to him, oh your mum doesn't trust me. But do you know what it was? Being brought up with grandparents, I was the ninth one they brought home. I had a lot of hand-me-downs and my babies weren't hand-me-downs they were mine, that's what it was.

So you had 8 brothers and sisters?

Well they weren't home with me because.
Well ... to speak honestly, I was their eldest daughter's mistake.
And in those days you went through a lot.

Some things weren't better in the past were they?

No but since I've been in Cirencester people have been lovely to me, in the shops and everywhere and at GCHQ. My grandmother was lovely but my grandfather was very strict. He was ashamed, he didn't want people to know what his daughter had done. The squire used to live near where we were and he used to say, our surname was Clarke, and he used to say, 'Clarke stop chastising that child.' Well I survived, I wouldn't give in. I'm in here with the pain but I'm determined to keep going as long as I can.

I was married to my first husband for 28 years.
He died of a tumour of the brain.
I was 47 when he died. It was a hard blow.

We were in Hong Kong and we had to fly home when he was dying.
I used to go and see him every day in the hospital. There was a young
man, he'd been injured, he was a young soldier. I think he used to like
me going to see my husband, and his bed was there and my husband's
was there, and I'd be like that holding both hands. We were living in
Hong Kong when he got ill. I was working in the school, helping out
at the school. The Chinese were good to me, ever so kind. It was an
education for my boys too, Phillip went to Kowloon School. In fact
Phillip was going back to teach there as a surprise for me but of course
his dad was taken ill and he had to cancel the job. We lived out there 6
years, we did 2 tours. My husband worked for GCHQ; there was a base
there. It's been handed back now hasn't it. We did have a lovely amah.
We didn't have one at first and all my boys were in lovely white shirts.
What I like about it was you could get such nice things and I sent them
back to my family. Do you remember car coats? We had such a lovely
amah but before that I said to my husband, well I'll do the work and
I'll have the amah's money. I knew a little bit of Chinese, mostly for
shopping and cooking like.

*So you came back to the UK with your children but your husband seriously
ill?*

Yes we came back to Dorset, after I lived around the hospitals a long
time in London. But I got a job and bought me own house. So I moved
from Dorset to Churchdown and I went to work at GCHQ. I worked
there for 17 years and they were lovely to me, really kind to me. Of
course you can always help people. I've never sat around so much as I
have in here, and I've had more food in one day than I have in a week.
When you're busy you can't always stop can you. Yes I was on my own
with my boys at first. So my first husband died in Dorset. You had to
walk a couple of miles into the village. I never did learn to drive. He

always used to say, there's no need for you to drive, I'll be here to look after you. And my second husband said the same. I should have learnt to drive. When I took the guest house I earned my husband a car in a month. It was hard work, I had lovely guests, from Nottingham and Lincoln, they used to come twice a year sometimes. We loved it there, just open the gate and across to the beach.

Then I met my second husband at GCHQ, he was 6 years asking me to go out with him. He'd lost his wife and I was a bit afraid for him slipping up with his work. And I had a feeling, I didn't want to be just a replacement. That was Tom and we had eight and a half years. He had cancer and I think he knew he had it before he told me because I was his secretary and he was supposed to bring his medical certificate to me and he said I've taken it straight to the office. So I said what was wrong with you then? He discharged himself straight out of the hospital, he wouldn't stay in there. And I found out it was prostate cancer and I think he had it before we was married. I wish he had, I would have looked after him. He worshipped my boys, he said they'd done more for him than his own child. He was strict with his own. He's lost his wife, 54 with a heart attack. So I used to chat with the man at the gym – no more trouble I said, I've had enough.

I used to go to the gym until I was 89.
Cross-country, the rowing machine.
I used to work off 300 calories.
And then have a cup of coffee with cream in.

Those gym lads were lovely to me.

The manager said I was all the youngsters surrogate mum. They've had a cake every year. With the high blood pressure when I was 89 my doctor said I don't know about you going to the gym anymore but another doctor, a lady doctor, said I should still go. I loved it but the cakes have taken over now, last Christmas I did 25. My son said it's too much mum, you've got to cut down. I did, by two. I haven't given in. You know those wheels you put your feet in like pedals and go round?

Well I sit in the bathroom and do that. And here I've been keeping on and moving.

They say I've got a leaky valve
and now they say the heart's damaged.
But these things come to try you don't they.

I was sent on a prescription from the doctor to the gym for 12 weeks because I had pneumonia and cardiac asthma. I really loved it. But I tripped over the aerobic machine and damaged my leg. I've damaged all kind of things, trimming bushes and all sorts. I've won prizes for my gardening. My daughter-in-law thought it was too much for me. But I said no, I've got to keep going. If I get depressed I start living in the past, thinking about the husbands and that doesn't do you any good. A lady at the gym said to me, you're lucky, my mother's only 70 and she can't do what you do. She sits and watches telly all day. Well I got fed up with it one day and I said, look if I didn't do what I do I would be the same. I know the other year when we had all that ice and snow I couldn't get about, I seized up and put on weight too. I don't like the dark days, every morning it just seems dark. It makes you miserable doesn't it.

When my second husband died I started going on holiday on my own. We went to Madeira on our honeymoon. He used to go to France in his caravan but after Madeira he wanted to go to other places. I went to the Algarve, it was difficult but it was good. I was a bit frightened at first but I met some nice people. A young man in the hotel said never mind, I'll look after you. So I went all over the place. Croatia, oh the waterfalls there. When I was at GCHQ I wasn't allowed, not Croatia or Turkey. I've been to quite a lot of places in Spain, I used to go every year. Last time I went abroad was thirteen years ago, that was Greece.

Are you alright Mary?
No I'm having trouble.
Shall I get somebody to help you?
Yes, that would be nice.
Ah hello, could you kindly help
me? I've slipped down.

You know since I've been on all these trips my memory's going a bit, I couldn't remember where it was, it was a lovely place. Twenty Four tablets a day. I wish I could remember that place. Near Crete, like Crete. I went on my own. I've had a full life, yes. The boys are educated. One's a deputy headmaster, he's a preacher now. They're all in their 60s now. Paul's an accountant and Colin was an engineer. And my youngest one worked on oil rigs. He does such a lot of driving and that worried me, I nearly lost him. He had a head-on collision and I had to fly out to Scotland. Both legs were broken, his head was bashed and he was burnt by his seatbelt. He was only 23. He recovered but his legs hurts him a lot. I tell him he ought to do less driving … but he's the parent and I'm the little child. It happens. You're stubborn mum, you won't do what you're told. No. I won't have people go teaching me back things I've already taught them.

*

Doris, when you think back to when you were young in the past, what have been the changes from then to now in the way people live?

Everything's changed. I don't think people are as strict now as they used to be. I bought my boys up strict. I think if you're relaxed it's for the best. I were awfully strict, I had to be running a guesthouse. When my little Clive was 3 I gave him some apple and pastry and he was trying to stretch the pastry across and one of the guest's said – Can't you get it straight son? You should get the hammer and flatten it. No, he said, I won't, that'll have germs. I ran the guesthouse for eight years, it helped my boys a lot. Sometimes I think the strictness we were brought up with then is better than now. If I was out after 9 the door was locked so I went off to my sister's and stayed with her, which upset my mum, I called her my mum, my Gran like.

*Noise of repeated heavy
hammering on pipes.*

28

I don't think this drummer's going to make it Doris.

No, he's only got one tune.

So, as you say a full life.

But you know I can remember some things. This squire who used to live near the village, he had two little dogs called Whisky and Soda. And nobody was allowed to touch them but I could stroke them. I used to open the farm gate in the morning, so he could go through without getting off his horse. He was lovely to me. Once I tried to copy my brother with the milk can, he could swing it without a drop coming out, I was only about 6 or 7. Well I tried it and it went all over me. The squire had his staff clean me up and put me in a little dress and everything. He knew about the situation with my grandparents, everybody knew.

I think he was keeping an eye on me.
I get people now saying, you had a terrible time.
But I was happy, I didn't notice, you don't do you.
If you're in it, you're in it.
Children are … they keep going.

I've got a new great grandson, he's not 2 until next April. He runs into everything and he's always banging his head, he cut his head the other day. When I did that the blood woke me up. I had to clean up the carpets the next day, my son told me off and took me to the hospital. Do you know that Vanish stuff?

Yes I do, it's very good, it works.

Well I mixed some of that up with water and it took it all out. And I'm very particularly about dishcloths, they must be snow white. I'm a big believer in that Vanish. It was my son that brought me here. Then he worried. I've got four sons, six grandchildren and five great grandchildren. Don't I know it at Christmas. I still make all the Christmas cakes for them, I did think one of the granddaughters would follow me in doing it. My sons were with the first husband, we were married too young really. I was married at 19, he was two years older than me. He used to go on courses a lot. I was in hospital after Clive was just born and he had to go on a twelve-week course. I could have done with him home with four children, especially when I'd just come home with a new baby. I think that's why the boys are so clinging with me – because I've been mother and father.

I better have a drink of water, I've got to be careful I don't faint. I've slid out the chair twice and fainted.

Let me get it for you.

Thank you very much. I'm sure if I'd been able to go to the gym, I wouldn't be in here. I don't know how long I'm going to be in here. They told my boys I'm very poorly, they worry so. My youngest one buys me all sorts of things. I say, don't spend your money on me Clive. Well he says, it's for all those dirty nappies you changed.

People used to say to me, oh you had a handful.
I didn't have a handful.
I loved them and it was a pleasure.
It wasn't a burden, it was a pleasure.
They were mine.
They weren't hand-me-downs.

I used to take them out a lot. I was very particular. My grandma, you've never known anyone so particular. She was a dressmaker. I've seen photographs of the children when they were little. The boys had grey trousers, maroon blouses, cream collars and cream cuffs. And the girls had maroon dresses with cream collars and cuffs. She had several little ones together you know, she had one every year.

You know, when I was young, it was church in the morning, Sunday school in the afternoon and chapel at night. And then later on I sang in the choir. A man called Cyril from London came and he wanted to take me back to London with him and have my voiced trained but you can imagine my grandfather can't you. I'm not paying for anything like that. He wasn't going to pay for that. Well I made my way despite that, that's what my boys say. My mother's name was Milly. It was better getting away. You get it all thrown back at you. It was a sin as far as my grandfather was concerned, he didn't want people to see me. He's not going to stop with that hammer is he?

> *Nurse can you help me?*
> *Beatrice?*
> *Nurse?*
> *Shall we have a*
> *little sit down?*
>
> *What's all that banging?*

What my... it'll come back in a few minutes. It's gone off worse here, my memory, since the tablets.

My grandmother used to take me to see my mother. Do you watch *Downton Abbey*? She worked in one of them places like that. She was taken advantage of, a kitchen girl. In that case, years ago, you got called bastard, hedge-bottomer, all sorts. It's not a good thing from the past. My first husband was so kind, I've never had anyone so kind. It wouldn't be classed as a sin these days.

Is that everything I've said, in the recording? The only thing to leave out is about being born before marriage. I've always been ashamed of that.

Well I don't think you should be but it's your feeling. So it's up to you Doris.

Yes, yes. That's what my cousin used to say. My grandfather shouldn't have been like he was because it's never the baby's fault. There's no more innocent thing than a baby. But I loved him. If anyone was after me he'd be there. Some girls after school were going to get me but he was out after them. It's always been like a tarnish.

After all these years, it's ridiculous Doris.

Yes, yes it is.

Look at what you've done with your life, the people you've brought up in the world.

I know, I know. Yes. And I think about my husbands, I have to think about both of them or I feel guilty. Can't just think about one. I wanted to be married, everyone else was getting married. That wasn't the recipe was it? It's like when I saw the doctor last year. He said I was an advert for other people. I'll keep going as long as I can. He said, what's your recipe? I said, keep smiling, keep working and a bit of wrinkle cream. I think I want a lot now! I won't give in. I keep having these attacks, I've got the spray. The pain's wicked, it feels like someone has stabbed you and poured boiling water on you. It's with every little exertion, like when I go to the toilet or I can't get comfortable on those mattresses. I just can't eat all the food.

Hello, here we are.
This is Michael.
Enjoy your lunch

I had a lot of hand
me downs and my babies
weren't hand me downs

they were mine

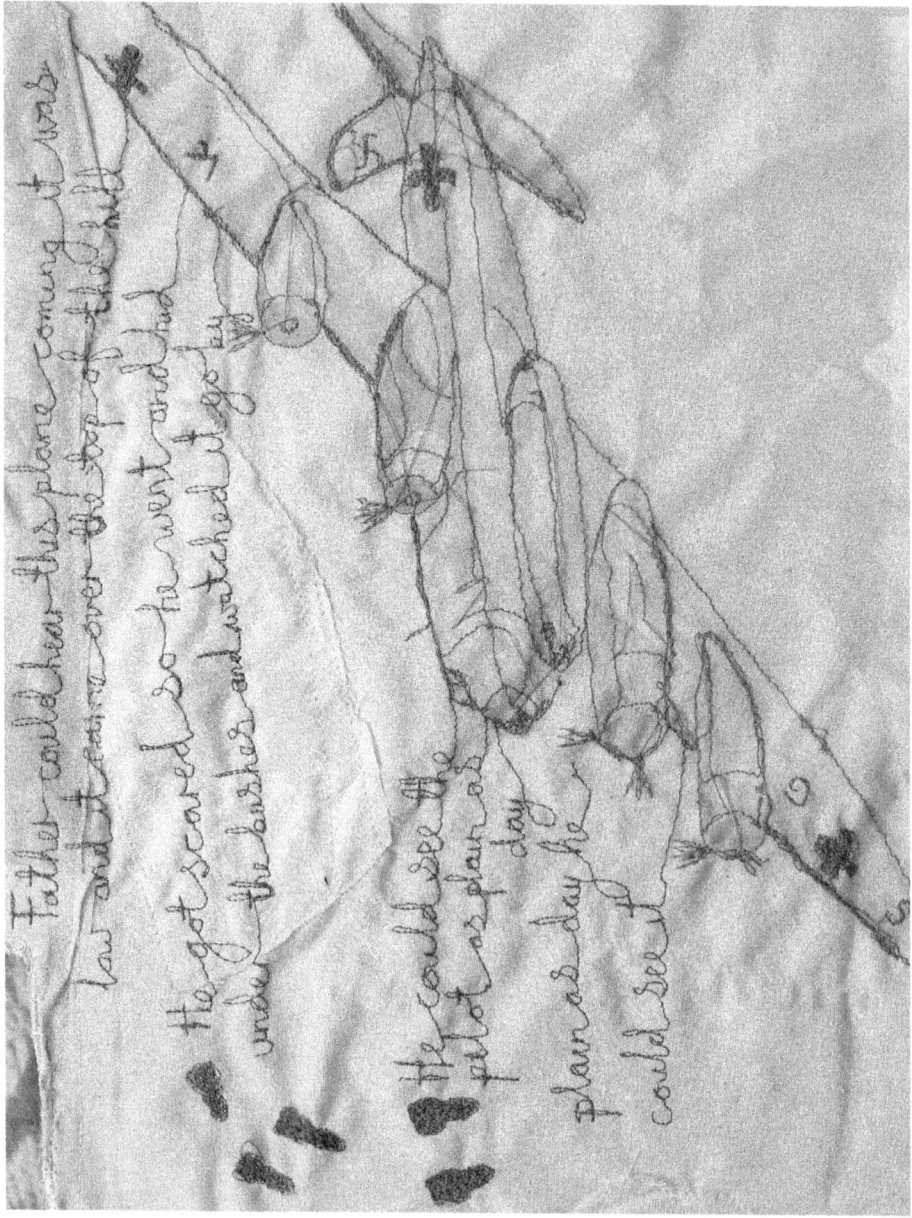

Father could hear this plane coming it was
low and it came over the top of the hill

He got scared so he went and hid
under the bushes and watched it go by

He could see the
pilot as plain as
day

plain as day he
could see it

John

I was born 1930 in Cheltenham. We lived on top of Leckhampton Hill. Hartley Top. Lived there 14 years. The old man, my dad, and my mother, they were married in June and I was born in October.

They were fond of each other we would say.

Yes, well, ha. As I say we lived there until I was 14 and then my brother was born. Dad worked on the farm, his dad was a farmer. We moved from there to Malmesbury, Wiltshire. He was head herdsman.

I 'em, yea, I've got some wipes. You got any pyjamas?

We were there for ten years and then we moved to Bracknell, Berkshire. That was about 1945, 1946. I finished school at 14 when we went to Malmesbury. My first job was on a farm, I was second herdsman with Hereford cattle. I moved about all over the place then, building. I came back to Cheltenham to get married. Her and her mother were friends of my mother.

So you'd known each other a long time?

It didn't last long though … we had one daughter … then … she left me.

I met another woman and we were together … 23 years.

Then she died and that was the end of that.

Then mum and dad retired and went to Ross-on-Wye.

They died … and my brother … and that left me on my own.

My daughter lives in Cheltenham. She's a lovely girl.

What's today? It's Monday I think. She won't be in today.

Our Susan, she's the pillar of my life as far as I'm concerned.

My daughter's got two, a boy and a girl. One's at university in Reading, the other I don't know what he's doing. He supposed to be going back to college. He wasted his last year, he's a fool. You have to be a fool now and again don't you. I think Owen, my grandson, he wishes now, I know he wishes now he could go back to college. He's saving up. He was studying law. I didn't see much of them when they were little. They were always in bed or at school when I went up there. It didn't bother me, all I was interested in was

Our Susan … she had a gorgeous smile, an absolutely gorgeous smile.

Oh when she was a kiddy in the pram in the garden.

*

So you were a teenager during the war then. Did you see anything of it?

Well more or less at night, when the German planes came over. The guns opened up from Brockworth. You could hear the shrapnel falling over the house. Father, he was down in the field one day and he could hear this plane coming. It was low and it came over the top of the hill, he reckoned it was no higher than twenty foot off the ground. He got scared so he went and hid under the bushes and he watched it go by. He could see the pilot as plain as day, plain as day he could see it. Don't know what happened to it afterwards.

What do you remember of your school days Mr J. ?

Ah. I started off at Coberley. Used to walk five or six fields to get to school. No buses, nothing like that. It was a good school actually, Coberley was. Then I went to Naunton Park in town. No I didn't like school. I hated it. I played truanted quite a lot. I never learnt a thing really. You never learn 'til you leave school and then you start.

You just think now, the attendance officer had to come all the way up to the top of Leckhampton Hill, all the way up Quarry Road, more or less across the fields to your house. I used to go out and meet him. 'Do you know where Mrs J. lives?' he said, 'Yes everyone knows where Mrs J. lives.' He'd say, 'Do you know a John J. ?' 'Yes.' He'd give me the letter and that was the last of it. School wasn't for me.

Holidays and weekends was best. I used to go rabbiting, setting wires, setting traps, ferreting, shooting, all sorts. I was out and about, a country boy. Definitely preferred that to being in school. Definitely. I've been rabbiting more or less all my life.

So you began working when you were 14?

On the farm, six in the morning 'til six at night. Milking the cows, twice a day. I used to go down there, sit underneath a white short-horn cow, tits, huge great tits on it. Used to take about half an hour. I was doing that when I was 12, before I left school. Then I became second herdsman. Then 10 years in Malmesbury, 10 years in a person's life that was.

You meet friends, you meet people. You get close and then you get married.

And then you lose them and you're back on your own all the time.

My Mrs and her mother came up to Bracknell, for a week I think it was. I said to Pat, I said – 'Will you marry me Pat?' I said. We were messing about in the cowshed. 'Yes.' she said. Straight away, no messing. I was 20. We got on well together. Two and a half years after our Susan was born the doctor sent me to hospital for a check-up. He said you've got a very bad heart.

Sorry to disturb you. Am I interrupting?
No, not at all.
Oh sorry I thought you were a relative.
Are you sure?
I'll come back next week.

He said I had a very bad heart. So I had to quit working on the building and I was out of work two and a half years then. We couldn't keep the house going.

It's a shame the way life goes.

The problem is I still love her

– because she's the mother of my daughter.

Then I went to see him again and he said – it's still very bad Mr J. And then I was going to get married again and went to see him. 'Mr J.,' he said, 'your heart's as strong as a lion. You'll live to be a 100.' I thought bloody hell, after I lost all that. You think of what I lost. Well if I had the heart he was on about, I wouldn't be here. There was nothing wrong with me.

All that waste of my life, especially when Pat left me.

That went on for twenty odd years. All that time.

When he told me that, eventually, I worked at Smith's. I stopped there, that was a good thing. Then I was made redundant and that was it. I had a pension. I only had a flat. It wasn't too bad. The only trouble is, with this I've got now, I've got a job to climb the stairs. This is the second time I've been in here. I don't know what trouble it is to be honest with you.

I suppose one of these days it'll be pop.

And that'll be the end of me.

Not really worried. Except for Susan.

Of course my mum and dad, they capitulated both of them. More or less on me own then. I've still got my brother, one cousin, two cousins – that's the way it is. I had one aunty, on my dad's side, she was 104, so I'm not doing too bad really.

George the only trouble is the physio's only just got you out haven't they?

Lord, yes, I still think about them, my parents.

I go back to Hartley, there, those days where I was born. We had photographs of me up there, ah I can see those photographs plain as day. Yep. A long time ago, a hell of a long time ago. Well you've saved me having to walk about on that zimmer. I don't mind I can walk on a zimmer, if I have to.

Have you got any pain anywhere?

*

Is time a healer do you think?

Time? No. But it can let you come back to life again. The only trouble is for me, I go back to the flat and I'm back to square one, the same environment. They're on about getting me to go somewhere else when I'm out. I don't like being in the side rooms, I don't like being on my own. There's not a lot going on here, just three old men besides me. But there is more going on, even sat here doing nothing.

This place is a great healer. They are trying hard to get me back on my feet again. I'll get back on my feet, oh I will eventually, pull myself together and help them out.

You can have a chat.

Well not exactly chat. I think they're like me, too old to chat. But it's nice talking to you actually. Very nice. It brought make memories.

I don't mean to upset you.

I know. I'll soon get over it. I'm always tired, I don't know why. The trouble is, I'm a weepy sort of person. When you start thinking about it, it makes you cry. It's nice to think of these things and talk about them. I've never talked about them before. Her name was Bernie Spencer, my mum, and my dad was Sidney. Sidney and Bernie and our John. The trouble they had with me too. That's one thing, he never hit me my dad, never. He hit my brother once, he smacked him on the leg once. It was a shotgun wedding. Kids used to say at school, do you know something, John J., you're a bastard. I know – and I'm proud of it too.

Shakespeare says, '...gods stand up for bastards.'

Now we know, with the space age and all the rest of it, we know there's no such thing as God. I'm a non-believer. Dad was a Methodist, mum was Church of England. When I went to school five days a week I couldn't see any sense in going on Sunday as well. I went once but I didn't go again. It wasn't for me. You work it out. This ISIS business, it's disgusting. They can only be as thick as two short planks.

That's the physio waiting for me. She's gone out now.

We'll carry on until she comes back, we can make something up.

I've never talked about them before

we got over the hoo ha — it caused

we were perfectly alright about it —

I think we argued over many things

but never that

Elizabeth

I was born July 1930 in Belfast. My family were living in County Down and my mother was whistled up in a motor car there by her brother-in-law to be, a young naval officer, who was much embarrassed when everyone at the nursing home thought him to be the father. She had the baby there but protested first of all, having sent one doctor away because he was too young, she told him to get lost. Yes, assertive I suppose but gentle as can be in other circumstances.

We all travelled over the sea for our education. I went to a place called North Foreland Lodge, I don't know what I learnt there, I just don't know. It was quite pleasant. We were in the Forest of Dean then, we were evacuated to there from the coast. On the whole it was quite fun. I liked the Forest very much. We were free to rush about anywhere, as long as there were three of us. One to fall down the hole, one to stay with her and the other to get help. It was a small school, only about eighty, all girls. We had a party once for the Americans, who had a miserable time. They all turned up and the girls had got themselves dressed up to the nines and we offered them a nice glass of lemonade. A kind thought but not perhaps what they had in mind.

Did I enjoy school? Well the truth of that matter is the bad bits stick and you forget the good bits. This was while the war was going on. We were made to be aware of the war. I remember at the end we were shown pictures of the concentration camps, horrible. And we learnt Churchill's speeches by heart, and well worth it. There were a few sad girls whose brothers had died. We lived on rations but I suspect the headmistress used to creep out at night and shoot the odd deer. There were horrid things called Marmite fritters, which we all loved. Don't know how you make them, wouldn't mind trying.

I had a sister who at 19 fell in love with the man she would marry. Before marriage you couldn't go and live near the person you loved if they were on actual service. That was a great annoyance to her. So she went to work in a factory for a time in the East End and that was horrid because people didn't accept her. So she worked in a factory and she also joined a unit called … H P Herbert ran it, she had a navy-like uniform. They sailed up and down the Thames and were directed to any hospital that was in need of help. She wasn't a nurse, she wasn't anything. She was fed by a charming prostitute who happened to be serving with her. They never had any money, well at least the prostitute didn't do too badly. I don't know what they did, awful conditions of the blitz, they just did whatever was needed. She married a man in Bomber Command, had a wretched time. And there was my brother, school seemed to squash it out of him. He went to the army at first, went through Sandhurst and then to Palestine after the war. Oh we made a mess didn't we?

But really Northern Ireland was our base because my grandmother lived there and sweetly housed us all as the need arose. Father was serving in the air force so grandparents became the stable home. She was a dear and we all thought of that as home although we all travelled a lot. It was there I met my husband, he was Catholic and I was a Prod. I met him at 17, married at 18 and we had a police guard when we married. We got over the hoo-ha it caused, we were perfectly alright about it. I think we may have argued over many things but never that.

> *Can I help you?*
>> *Are you ok?*
> *I'm ok.*
>> *I hear you're going home.*
> *Not until tomorrow.*

Oh I was a little unfair, I was angry a bit. I've been kept here for days and days and days.

So, well, he agreed to be married in my church because my brides-maids wouldn't agree to go to his church. We thought all this was non-sense, I think we were quite right. So when we had children, no hang on, I'm jumping a gun. He married me in my church so he was unable to go to confession. So I thought, I'll put that right. I organised a little wedding, just a few friends, in the evening. Nobody knew, not even him. And we got him there, right to the church. So far it's worked very well … oh he's gone but … it worked very well on the whole. He was all of 27 when I married him.

Just as well. We had no money at all. I think we got £30 a month
to live on, not a lot. We went to Gibraltar and he could eat in the
mess but I couldn't, so I had a Crunchie for lunch. Once I carried one
home in triumph to find it was part of the shop display, it was wood.
Service in Gibraltar was good in patches but the lack of money, we had
to count everything. Do I sound ungrateful? The Navy used to come
in, they gave us dinner, which was nice. I enjoyed Gibraltar, I think. I
had two dresses, which I wore alternately, actually there was not much
difference. We lived in a flat where salt water came out of the taps, hot
salt water, which is sticky, and which is not good to bathe in. We had a
table, two chairs and a bed. Tony was a captain with the regiment and
the regiment goes from rather grand to absolute penury.

Six months there and then Germany and that's when life became
easier. It was lovely. We had horses that we rode. Help in the house.
We had everything. He was working for, I've forgotten the name of it,
wait a minute. The British Mission to the Soviet Forces. To his delight
he took to that. Once they caught him being in the wrong place and
they took him in and they had a horrible woman to interview him. She
said, do you speak German, French? No. Perfectly true, he didn't. Well
what did you learn at school? Latin. Ha! I went to a party given by the
Russians, having a jolly time. They must have been speaking English
or easy German, I spoke a little, yes easy German I think. They were
saying, the spy is in the kitchen, the spy is in the kitchen. They thought
I was the spy, not Tony. Amused me, annoyed Tony.

We had a system, if he got into trouble he would ask to see a Russian
officer, not a German. The *entente cordiale* was between the Russians
and us and not between the Germans and us. Some of the Germans
would try to frighten you on purpose. We had two trips to Germany.
My first boy was born there and my second son in Armagh, we were in
the barracks. I quite enjoyed it there, an enormous house, a beautiful
Georgian house, half of the Mess. If you'd had the money it would have
been such fun to do it up.

I want to go home.
Are you listening to me?
I want to go home.

We did what we could, Aunt Mabel's curtains and a few other handy gifts from family. It was fun in a peaceful sort of way. That was Bruno's time to arrive. After that we went back to Germany again, that was when Guy was born? Yes it was, I think. My timings get a little wobbly. You know I got on rather well with the Russians in Berlin. Once they have a drink in their hands and they're at a party they're inclined to enjoy themselves and they love singing their village songs. I remember one night we all behaved rather badly, drinking and hoolie, and some songs were sung. We made friends which you're told not to, in a nice English way – but we did. There was Grischel, I remember and he, it was so sad. His son was ill, he was dying. Poor old Grischel was heartbroken and he came to our medics to see if the matter was right. There was nothing could be done, they were right. All he wanted to do was fish. We went three times to Germany and Tony was happy as long as his job was interesting enough. With the regiment we had lots of fun, lots of lovely parties, wonderful parades – don't how much work anyone did. We had horses to ride. I used to ride as a girl, my sister tied me on to the saddle and that was it.

After that back to Northern Ireland. The hotel used to give dances. In Newcastle. What was the name of it? No good. Memory gone. It has too, over lots of things, how silly. A huge hideous red-brick thing on the seafront. It will still be a hotel. There was a rather naughty drunken man who owned the rights to their water and gas and when he was cross with them, which he often was, he would turn it off. Honestly my memory has worn itself out. Armagh is rather beautiful. How long were we there? You know I'm not sure. And I've no Tony to ask, sadly. This was the arrival of Bruno. He's 58 now I think. He was born in the local nursing home and next to me was a Catholic mother. I said, for God's sake, let us make an agreement that our sons will never fight each other, and she said OK. Then Guy was born. And we had one daughter but we lost her, I don't know where we were. In Germany. You see, ah, memory's gone. Slieve Donard was the name of that hotel.

So was Germany the last posting?

Yes the Russian was the last, four years of that for an officer who can't speak any languages was pretty damn lucky but he knew how to get around Germany in a motorcar. An interesting job, get out and look at all the bits you were not allowed, seeing what was there. He used to sleep out in the forest in midwinter and I sent him off with a great pack of food. He loved it. I don't think it's any secret anymore. A little while ago I wouldn't have, nobody talked about it very much. There was a plan. All the other families were going to be evacuated but we weren't, the reasoning was it would start a panic. So that was the last posting. I was very lucky really.

Oh and we went to Bangkok after that, I'd forgotten about that. I thought it was going to be lovely but I hated it. I usually settled into a place at once but Bangkok defeated me. I just … we lived in a compound. We had help, a darling woman. It should have been alright but it wasn't. I met a young American, the son of somebody. I joined up with him and we went to the immigration prison and there we discovered so many sad stories. And we decided we had to spring 'em. And we did. The Thais were quite happy to see them go if somebody paid. They were in prison for not having a passport. They had run away from Burma, with good reason and then settled down happy as could be, just pay the police the dosh every week. When they ran out of dosh – *plumpf* into prison. So we found a couple who were working for … I don't know what they were working for, they were Americans. They were doing wicked things like making pretend passports, having them beautifully printed. So they made a handful of pale blue ones with lovely gold writing for us to give to the men. And that worked beau-tifully. The agreement was that we would pay the airfare to get them over the border and they were not to come back but a lot of them did I'm afraid, they must have been better off there. The passports were very beautiful, I wish I'd kept one.

So this was not the reason you were in Thailand of course, to spring illegal immigrants?

No. No – but it was something I could do and keep myself occupied. We bought fruit and vegetables, they had nothing like that, just fish heads. Did Tony know? Ha. He got a bit het up and marched me to the ambassador. He said, look what's she's doing and I can't stop her. But the ambassador was sweet and said she hasn't done any harm, and when she goes we'll set up a proper prison visiting system. Whether they did or not I don't know, it was his intention. Some of the prisoners were so pathetic.

So your boys were at school during this time?

Yes. They all went to boarding school, that was the only way we could do it but I don't think I would do it again. Bruno went to the international school in Singapore and he blossomed.

<table>
<tr><td></td><td>I said why are you ignoring me? I want to see my doctor.</td></tr>
<tr><td></td><td>You're sat on somebody else's bed.</td></tr>
<tr><td></td><td>I don't give a damn. Come and sit in your room.</td></tr>
<tr><td>I'm so proud of my children.</td><td>Oh she's got one on her today.</td></tr>
<tr><td>Poor thing.</td><td>Cover your ears.</td></tr>
</table>

Well one went into the army and Bruno went to America – but he comes back very often. He works there for Neiman Marcus. And Guy looked after his father until he died and then he looked after me. A happy family, very. And I've got six grandchildren all from Simon. He married twice. First time was a bit of a disaster but he's very content now. I must stop talking. You've got some sort of switch that makes people talk.

I wouldn't know.

Yes, yes you have.

Well it's very interesting for me and I'm really pleased that you've been happy to talk.

I think I've run out of brain power.

I think there's plenty there. Let's just hope the Thai authorities don't read the account of you springing the prisoners.

Ha, ha – that was satisfactory, that was.

Thank you very much for giving me your time. It's been a pleasure talking to you.

Oh not at all. I've bored the boots off you for ages.

Not at all, away with you, as we would say.

we had to count everything

we had a table two chairs and a bed

NESTLÉ'S CRUNCH MILK CHOCOLATE

we had no money at all
I think we got thirty pounds to live on
we went to Gibraltar and he could
eat in the mess but I couldn't so I had a
crunchy for lunch   once I carried one
home in triumph to find it was part of
the shop display   it was wood

six months there   and then
Germany   and that's when
life became easier
it was lovely

A Chorus

i I was born in.

Joan
Jim George Tony and then me.
but that wasn't the finish
after I was born
there was Mari, John and little Alan.

I couldn't learn properly
I couldn't take things in
it regrets me still

I was 14 when I left school
left on the Friday, work on the Monday.

> *Doris*
> I was the ninth one they brought home,
> I had a lot of hand-me-downs.
>
> I'd passed the scholarship but I was brought up
> by my grandfather and he wouldn't let me go
> to the grammar school, he didn't believe in it.
> So I left at 14 and went to work.
>
> Well ... to speak honestly,
> I was their eldest daughter's mistake.
> And in those days you went through a lot.
>
> Well I made my way despite that,
> that's what my boys say.

But I was happy, I didn't notice, you don't do you.
If you're in it, you're in it.
Children are ... they keep going.

It's never the baby's fault.

'Clarke stop chastising that child.'

> *John*
> The old man, my dad, and my mother,
> they were married in June
> and I was born in October.
>
> No I didn't like school. I hated it.
> I played truant quite a lot.
> I never learnt a thing really.
>
> You could hear the shrapnel falling over the house.
> Father, he was down in the field one day
> and he could hear this plane coming.
> It was low and it came over the top of the hill,
> it was no higher than twenty foot off the ground.
>
> It was a shotgun wedding. Kids used to say at school,
> do you know something John you're a bastard.
> I know – and I'm proud of it too.
>
> I used to go rabbiting, setting wires, setting traps,
> ferreting, shooting, all sorts.
> I was out and about, a country boy.

Joan
Of course the war was on
we all caught head lice,
mum soon got rid of it.

Elizabeth
She had the baby there but protested first of all,
having sent one doctor away because he was too
young,
she told him to get lost. Yes, assertive I suppose
but gentle as can be in other circumstances.

We all travelled over the sea for our education.
I don't know what I learnt there, I just don't know.
It was quite pleasant.

We had a party once for the Americans,
the girls had got themselves dressed up to the nines
and we offered them a nice glass of lemonade.
A kind thought but not perhaps what they had in
    mind.

I remember at the end we were shown pictures
of the concentration camps, horrible.
And we learnt Churchill's speeches by heart.

We had horses to ride. I used to ride as a girl,
my sister tied me on to the saddle and that was it.

Doris
'Clarke stop chastising that child.'

ii Will you marry me?

Joan
I met my husband when I was 17
he came from Yorkshire
we lived in a cottage on the estate
we wrote to each other and got married

No we never had children in the end
I just didn't, they didn't catch on
I enjoyed my sister's
I loved her little one.

> *Doris*
> And then in 1942 I married my first husband
> And then I had 3 in 7 years 2 months.
> And all my boys were in lovely white shirts.
> Philip went to Kowloon School.
>
> People used to say to me, oh you had a handful.
> I didn't have a handful.
> I loved them and it was a pleasure.
> It wasn't a burden, it was a pleasure.

Joan
No we never had children in the end.

> *Doris*
> I've got four sons, six grandchildren
> and five great grandchildren.
>
> My first husband was so kind,
> I've never had anyone so kind.

John
I said to Pat, I said –'Will you marry me Pat?' I said.
'Yes.' she said. Straight away, no messing.
I was 20. We got on well together.

Our Susan … she had a gorgeous smile,
an absolutely gorgeous smile.
Oh when she was a kiddy
in the pram in the garden.

Elizabeth
I met my husband, he was Catholic and I was a Prod.
I met him at 17, married at 18
and we had a police guard when we married.
I think we may have argued over many things
but never that.

So far it's worked very well … oh he's gone but …
it worked very well on the whole. He was all of 27
when I married him.

He was born in the local nursing home
and next to me was a Catholic mother.
I said, for God's sake, let us make an agreement
that our sons will never fight each other
and she said ok.

Bruno went to the international school in Singapore
and he blossomed.

iii A Crunchie for lunch

Joan
I was working but for very little money, oh dear, 1/6d an hour,
we never got in debt
He got £5 a week, which was nothing.

I was there 48 years
and I enjoyed it all.

My wench, he said, don't you get buying anything, he said,
unless you can afford it because it will get you into trouble.

> *Doris*
> We lived out there Hong Kong for six years,
> we did two tours. There was a base there.
> I knew a little bit of Chinese,
> mostly for shopping and cooking like.
>
> So I ran a guest house,
> so they didn't go short of anything.
> Five in the morning to eleven or twelve at night
> but it was for my boys and husband.
>
> I used to go to the gym until I was 89.
> Cross-country, the rowing machine.
> I used to work off 300 calories.
>
> > *John*
> > My first job was on a farm,
> > I was second herdsman with Hereford cattle.
> > I moved about all over the place then, building.
> >
> > > She was fed by a charming prostitute
> > > who happened to be serving with her.

They never had any money, well at least
the prostitute didn't do too badly.

I don't know what they did,
awful conditions of the blitz,
they just did whatever was needed.

We had no money at all. I think we got £30 a month
to live on, not a lot. We went to Gibraltar
and he could eat in the mess but I couldn't,
so I had a Crunchie for lunch.

He was working for, I've forgotten the name of it,
wait a minute – The British Mission to the Soviet Forces.

They thought I was the spy not Tony.
Amused me, annoyed Tony.

After that we went back to Germany again,
that was when Guy was born? Yes it was, I think.
My timings get a little wobbly.

Oh and we went to Bangkok after that,
I'd forgotten about that.
We went to the immigration prison
and there we discovered so many sad stories.
And we decided we had to spring 'em. And we did.

They were doing wicked things
like making pretend passports,
having them beautifully printed.

iv And that was the end of that.

Joan
We said, oh don't let him go back,
don't let him go back again,

Alan died at 14 months
what it was it was terrible, terrible
times doesn't, no it never does.

I don't think they're ever, when I say gone,
we know they're gone, it's the same with mum and dad
I still talk to mum and dad, when I go down to the graves,
the stones like, I'm always talking to them.

> *Doris*
> Yes. And I think about my husbands,
> I have to think about both of them or I feel guilty.
> Can't just think about one.
>
> My first husband died of a brain tumour,
> I was 47 when he died.
> We were in Hong Kong.

> > *John*
> > You meet friends, you meet people.
> > You get close and then you get married.
> > And then you lose them
> > and you're back on your own all the time.
> >
> > I met another woman we were together 23 years,
> > then she died and that was the end of that.
> >
> > Of course my mum and dad,
> > they capitulated both of them.

Elizabeth
How long were we there? You know I'm not sure.
And I've no Tony to ask, sadly.

So far it's worked very well … oh he's gone but …
it worked very well on the whole.

v But he's the parent.

Joan
Of course they had their children
and they still come to see me

I loved her little one and took him everywhere
my other sister had two boys,
and the children from the manor.

> *Doris*
> But he's the parent and I'm the little child, it happens.
> You're stubborn mum, you won't do what you're told.
> No. I won't have people go teaching me back things
> I've already taught them.
>
> The boys are educated. One's a deputy headmaster,
> he's a preacher now. They're all in their 60s.
> Paul's an accountant and Colin was an engineer.

> *John*
> Our Susan, she's the pillar of my life
> as far as I'm concerned.

> *Elizabeth*
> I'm so proud of my children.
> And I've got six grandchildren.

John
The pillar of my life.

vi I suppose one of these days.

Joan
They've gone now, there's only John, my younger sister
and me that's living now…

I still talk to mum and dad, when I go down to the graves,
the stones like, I'm always talking to them.

> *Doris*
> The pain's wicked, it feels like…
> someone has stabbed you
> and poured boiling water on you.
>
> What my … it'll come back in a few minutes.
> It's gone off worse here, my memory, since the tablets.
>
> But I said no, I've got to keep going. If I get depressed
> I start living in the past, thinking about the husbands
> and that doesn't do you any good.
>
> He said, what's your recipe?
> I said keep smiling, keep working
> and a bit of wrinkle cream.
> I think I want a lot now!

> > *John*
> > I suppose one of these days it'll be pop.
> > And that'll be the end of me.
> > Not really worried, except for Susan.
> >
> > The pillar of my life.
> >
> > Lord, yes, I still think about them, my parents.
> > I go back to Hartley, there, those days where I was born.

We had photographs of me up there,
ah I can see those photographs plain as day.

Sidney and Bernie and our John.
The trouble they had with me too.

This place is a great healer. They are trying hard
to get me back on my feet again.
I'll get back on my feet, oh I will eventually,
pull myself together and help them out.

Elizabeth
No good. Memory gone. It has too,
over lots of things, how silly.

Honestly my memory has worn itself out.
Armagh is rather beautiful. How long were we
    there?
You know I'm not sure.

Slieve Donard was the name of that hotel.

John
Not really worried, except for Susan.

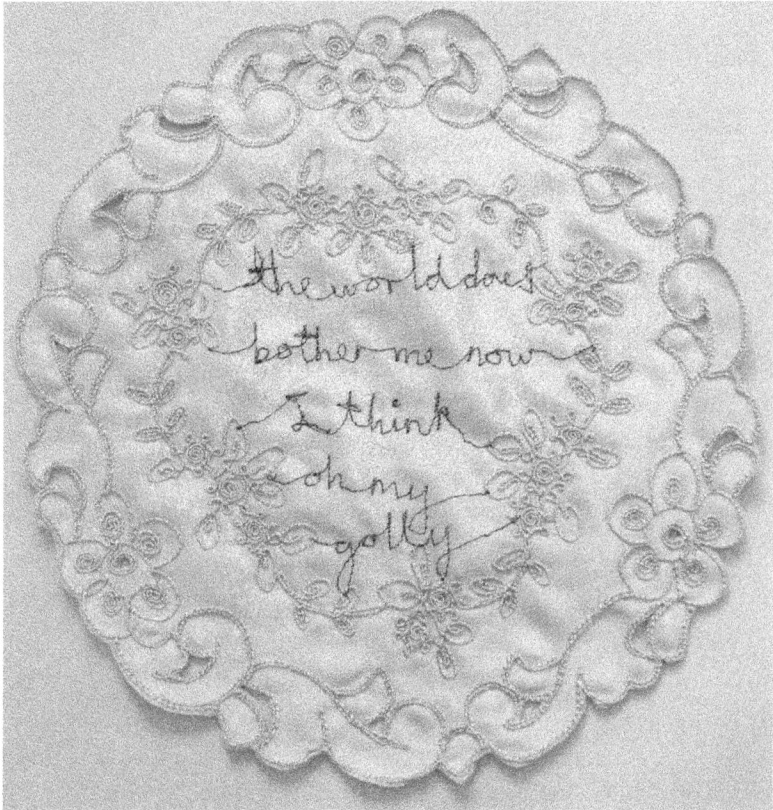

BIOGRAPHICAL NOTES

EMMA COLLINS

Emma is a textile artist, whose work mainly explores the interface between art and medicine. She strongly believes that art can inform the practice of medicine, just as the intricate factors that feed into medicine can become the subject of art. In 2011, Emma took a break from her medical career to complete a foundation diploma in art and design in Stroud.

Emma mostly works with fabrics, found objects, free-style machine stitching and hand embroidery. These often time consuming, traditional processes suit the narrative context of her work.

Emma works in South Wales as a GP and palliative-care doctor, as well as continuing to make art.

KELVIN CORCORAN

Kelvin Corcoran lives in Brussels. He has published numerous books of poetry and been anthologised in the U.K. and the U.S.A. His most recent book is *Facing West* (2017). *New and Selected Poems* is available from Shearsman Books, along with three major collections: *Backward Turning Sea* (2008), *Hotel Shadow* (2010) and *Sea Table* (2015). In addition he has interviewed Lee Harwood for the volume *Not the Full Story: Six Interviews with Lee Harwood*, published in 2008. *For The Greek Spring*, a selection of Kelvin Corcoran's poetry about Greece, was published in 2013. *The Writing Occurs as Song: A Kelvin Corcoran Reader*, edited by Andy Brown, was published in 2013. Other recent work includes reading tours of the UK, performances and recording of the CD *A Thesis on the Ballad* with the Jack Hues Quartet, and collaborations with the pianist Sam Bailey.